To Joi

Jesus loves you,

Vernell Hightower

Transforming
POWER

Vernell Hightower

Gazelle
PRESS

ISBN 1-58169-152-1
For Worldwide Distribution
Printed in the U.S.A.

Gazelle Press
P.O. Box 191540 • Mobile, AL 36619
800-367-8203

Table of Contents

Acknowledgments

To God be the glory!

I thank the Lord for my husband, Tyrone Hightower, daughter, Lakeia Tameka Holmes for their encouragement and support throughout the many months of preparation of this book. I also thank my son and stepdaughter for just being a blessing. I thank my two mothers in the Lord, and my precious sisters in Christ for their enthusiasm in telling me to write until the Holy Spirit says to stop. God bless all of my family members and all who will pick up this book. To God be the glory.

To Mother

I just want to take this time to say thank you mother. You have welcomed my faith in Jesus Christ, and you have been very supportive of my new life in Jesus Christ. I pray God's abundance your way today and everyday in Jesus holy name. I pray that you will become all that God is calling you to become in him. God bless you mother!

Introduction

This book contains messages of love to the loveless, grace to the fallen, hope to the hopeless, life to the spiritually dead, freedom from past failures and mistakes, healing to the hurting, strength to the weak, food to the hungry, water to the thirsty, and vision to the visionary. One word from God can make the difference!

> *Sing praises to God, sing praises: Sing praises unto our King, sing praises. For God is the King of all the earth: Sing ye praises with understanding. God reigneth over the heathen: God sitteth upon the throne of his holiness* (Psalm 47:6-8).

To the reader, who is loved by a loving and merciful God who wants you to know that He is thinking about you! God knows you and has a great plan for your life. No matter where you are or what you have done, God's forgiveness is available to you. As you read this book, I pray that you will be blessed and encouraged to allow Jesus Christ to be Lord of your life. I pray that you will open up your heart to the gospel of Jesus Christ if you have not made that most crucial decision. I pray that you will allow God's Holy Spirit to transform your life for God's glory. We have a Savior and His name is Jesus Christ.

The Apostle Paul wrote, "Brethren, I count not myself to have apprehended: but this one thing I do, forgetting those things which are behind, and reaching forth unto those things which are before" (Philippians 3:13).

You and I like the Apostle Paul are still not what we should be, but we must forget those things which are behind and keep grabbing forth of those things which are before us. The Apostle Paul said,

Looking unto Jesus the author and finisher of our faith; who for the joy that was set before him endured the cross, despising the shame, and is set down at the right hand of the throne of God (Hebrews 12:2).

We must look to Jesus Christ because what God starts, He will finish. So we have to look to the author and finisher of our faith. "Being confident of this very thing, that he which hath begun a good work in you will perform it until the day of Jesus Christ" (Philippians 1:6).

We do not have to stay in our pain or past failures. We do not have to allow our past to dictate our future. God has provided a way out. What is that way? Jesus Christ is the only way. Jesus Christ came to set the captives free.

So many people are hurting, wounded, oppressed, depressed, and empty. They are searching in all the wrong places looking for satisfaction, peace, and security that sometimes takes us on a long self destructive path. As long as we put other people and things before God, we will always have unmet needs. These self destructive ways will destroy our lives, and kill our dreams. Set your heart to seek the Lord God Almighty.

"When thou saidst, Seek ye my face; my heart said unto thee, Thy face, Lord, will I seek" (Psalm 27:8).

Chapter 1

A New Life

Although my story is not unique, it does demonstrate how great is the love of God for each one of us. I never experienced what society calls the "traditional family" because my parents were unmarried and very young at the time of my birth, and I was raised by my great aunt. Many of my aunts, uncles, and grandparents chipped in to help raise me, but by the time I was 13, I ran away from home. During that time, I started popping Valium, taking speed, drinking alcohol, and smoking pot, trying to fill the void in my life.

That same year I became pregnant and gave birth to a beautiful baby girl, whom I named Rockquel. She was born with heart problems, and by the time my baby was 2 1/2 months old, she had two open heart surgeries. One month after her second surgery, she was released from the hospital and was doing well. Suddenly, a couple months later, Rockquel began burning up with a fever so I called her private doctor and told him about it. I followed his instructions to give her some Tylenol with orange juice and made an appointment to bring her into his office first thing in the morning. I got up around 5:00 a.m. and went over to her to find out why she had not awakened for her middle-of-the-night feeding. When I touched her, she felt cold. I quickly turned on the light and discovered that my beautiful baby girl had passed away in her sleep. I shouted, I screamed, and I cried, "Why God?"

I had to watch my baby girl be carried out of the house in a little black box. Although I experienced the death of my baby at such an early age, now I thank God that Rockquel did not have to grow up suffering with serious heart problems.

As the months passed, I became more lonely and distraught. At the time of Rockquel's death I was pregnant and five months later gave birth to another beautiful baby girl whom I named Lakeia. During this pregnancy, I stayed away from drugs and alcohol, but afterwards I went back to popping pills, drinking alcohol, and smoking pot. I was looking for satisfaction in all the wrong relationships, places, and things. I was looking for something to take away my pain and make me feel normal. I always felt like something was missing in my life, so I turned to drugs and negative relationships, trying to find fulfillment and relief.

Behold, I was shapen in iniquity, and in sin did my mother conceive me. Behold, thou desirest truth in the inward parts; and in the hidden part thou shalt make me to know wisdom (Psalm 51:5-6).

At the age of 16, I had my own apartment. I wanted to do the right thing, but it just seemed as though the more I tried, the more I failed. At the age of 17, I gave birth to a handsome baby boy. After my son's birth, I still continued to indulge and experiment with drugs.

I began to experience the party life at that time. I

was introduced to acid, and every weekend I went to a party, disco, or a bar. I was also in an abusive relationship and had a gun put to my head twice. It is only by the grace of God that I am alive to write about all of this. I know now, as I look back, God was watching over me in the midst of my self-destructive lifestyle. Thank You, Lord, for Your angels that encamped around me. Thank You, Lord, for Your love, grace, mercy, and protection.

The Enemy Moved In

I did graduate from high school and received my diploma. Instead of going to college, I continued pursuing the party life. The following year, I was attending a party with some girlfriends, and that night I was introduced to cocaine. My friends were passing the mirror, along with the cocaine and the straw. When I was asked if I wanted to sniff a little bit, I refused. I remember saying that I would never go that far with drugs. But when you are out in the world, serving your flesh and the devil, all of your "Nevers" eventually become "Yes, I will just try a little bit." It starts out through your curiosity and desire to have some fun. Next thing you know, you are addicted. The "get high" game isn't a game any longer.

Two years later after my introduction to cocaine, I was introduced to heroin, and that white powder became my way of escape. I was hurting inside and did not know why. For the most part, I felt unsatisfied and unfulfilled. I wanted help, but did not know who to turn to for help. I tried to look like I had it all together, but I was deteriorating inside. I wanted to numb my feelings because I was hurting. I welcomed the false high for the moment. After the high wore off, reality looked me right back in the face. I did not like what I had done to my life, and what I had become. Later, after the Lord saved me, I was reading my Bible, and the Holy Spirit showed me first Peter 5:8, "Be sober, be vigilant; because your adversary the devil as a roaring lion, walketh about, seeking whom he may devour." This scripture from the word of God showed me that Satan was out seeking to devour me. I found out that I had an adversary helping me to self destruct.

Also I read John 10:10, "The thief cometh not but for to steal, and to kill, and to destroy." This adversary, the devil, wanted to destroy me, and I was cooperating with him because I put his poison into my body. Thank God for His only begotten Son Jesus Christ. John 10:10 also says, "I am come that they might have life, and that they might have it more abundantly." Jesus came to give us life, and life more abundantly.

During the time of my drug addiction, I quit my job, pawned jewelry, TVs, VCRs, and sold food stamps. I was in bondage in every sense of the word. I felt sick, helpless, and hopeless. I tried methadone, a drug that addicts use in place of drugs to wean themselves off their drug addiction. I bought it from people who were in the drug treatment programs., but that did not work for me either. Everyday I would say to myself, *This is the last time.* I thought I was going to lose my mind. Depression, oppression, and low self-esteem became a big part of my life.

One day I remember my grandmother holding my hand and saying, "I am praying for you." "The effectual fervent prayer of a righteous man availeth much"

(James 5:16). My great aunt also was praying for me during that time. Neither one of them told me that they knew about my drug problem, but I guess they could tell by the company I kept.

During this period, a neighbor looked me right in my face and told me that Jesus Christ loved me. I did not know anything about Jesus Christ, but I remember smiling and feeling good inside when I heard His name. There is power in that name; there is life in that name; there is deliverance in that name. It was one of the few times I remember feeling good.

Many days I sat and looked out of my bedroom window and wondered why I was ever born. I went to sleep some nights wishing that I would never wake up, but the fact that I had two children always brought me back to reality. I knew I had to live because of them. I went to see a therapist and explained to him that I needed help. I figured that I must be mentally ill to keep putting poison in my system to numb my feelings. This doctor told me that I wasn't crazy, but knew exactly what I was doing. So I made an appointment with another doctor who told me that I had a chemical imbalance and prescribed some pills for me. I took the pills along with the drugs that I bought on the street. I remember crying out to God and saying, "God please help me. I am tired and cannot continue this destructive cycle; I need Your help."

A New Life Begins

"O wretched man that I am. Who shall deliver me from the body of this death?" (Romans 7:24). Who? I remember one morning a T.V. minister came on the screen and said, "Jesus Christ died for a sinner like you. Jesus went to the cross for a dope addict like you." He pointed his finger at me and told me to say the sinner's prayer because Jesus Christ wants to set me free. I repeated every word that the minister told me to repeat.

I said, "Lord Jesus, I believe You went to Calvary cross for my sins. Lord Jesus forgive me for all of the sins that I committed against You. Lord Jesus, I believe that You rose on the third day from the dead to set me free and to give me eternal life. Thank you, Jesus Christ. I receive You into my heart right now in Jesus' holy name. Amen."

I followed the instructions from the pastor on the television, and that was the beginning of my walk with Jesus Christ 15 years ago. I praise God for His delivering power. Jesus Christ is truly the Savior of the world.

That day changed my entire future. The next Sunday I went to church and have never turned back to my old way of living. Everything started changing. I attended a Bible study whenever the doors of the church were opened and began fellowshipping with other born-again Christians. I became very active in the body of Christ. The Lord forgave my sins and gave me a fresh new start. I was instantly delivered from drugs, alcohol, and fornication (sex outside of marriage).

I discovered that abiding in Christ is vital in order for us to be fruitful and healthy. "Jesus said, If ye abide in me, and my words abide in you, ye shall ask what ye will, and it shall be done unto you" (John 15:7).

A couple of years later, I met my husband in church, and we have been married for more than ten years. I thank the Lord for my husband; he is a gift from the

Lord. We both are involved in the substance abuse ministry at our church, and I am also a part of the women's prison ministry.

The Battle Began

My mind went through some major battles. I wanted to think right and do right, but my mind was still trying to hold onto negative thoughts. The mind is Satan's battleground. I had lived a life of deception and lies for a long time and therefore needed God to teach me how to reprogram my mind. God began to show me how to be equipped with His Word so that I could cast down everything that is not of him. "Casting down imaginations, and every high thing that exalteth itself against the knowledge of God and bringing into captivity every thought to the obedience of Christ" (II Corinthians 10:5).

> *Finally my brethren, be strong in the Lord, and in the power of his might. Put on the whole armor of God, that ye may be able to stand against the wiles of the devil. For we wrestle not against flesh and blood, but against principalities, against powers, against the rulers of the darkness of this world, against spiritual wickedness in high places* (Ephesians 6:10-12).

We must put on the whole armor of God daily because we have an enemy who wants to destroy us and steal our new identity in Christ. Our flesh is also our enemy because our flesh wants to seek satisfaction in all the wrong things. Apostle Paul wrote,

For I know that in me [that is my flesh] *dwelleth no good thing; for to will is present with me; but how to perform that which is good I find not. For the good that I would I do not; but the evil which I would not, that I do. Now if I do that I would not, it is no more I that do it, but sin that dwelleth in me* (Romans 7:18-20).

For I delight in the law of God after the inward man. But I see another law in my members, warring against the law of my mind, and bringing me into captivity to the law of sin which is in my members (Romans 7:22-23).

Satan lied to me for many years. He knows our weaknesses and fears and will capitalize on them. The devil does not play fair; he plays dirty because he is out to destroy us. He wants us to be his puppets, but we do not have to submit to him. He watches us to find out our appetites, trying to seduce us, but we do not have to take his bait (which could be a man, woman, or the acts of lying, cheating, adultery, or homosexual behavior, pride, etc.) because Jesus gives us divine power to resist Satan's lies and temptations.

Don't be beguiled. Satan comes to steal, kill, and destroy. In Genesis we see that Adam, Eve, and their son Cain took the bait.

And the serpent said unto the woman, ye shall not surely die. For God doth know that in the day ye eat thereof, then your eyes shall be opened, and ye shall be as gods, knowing good and evil.

And when the woman saw that the tree was good for food, and that it was pleasant to the eyes, and a tree to be desired to make one wise, she took of the fruit thereof, and did eat, and gave also unto her husband with her; and he did eat (Genesis 3:4-6).

And the Lord said unto Cain, why art thou wroth? And why is thy countenance fallen? If thou doest well, shalt thou not be accepted? And if thou doest not well, sin lieth at the door, and unto thee shall be his desire, and thou shalt rule over him. And Cain talked with Abel his brother: and it came to pass, when they were in the field, that Cain rose up against Abel his brother, and slew him. And the Lord said unto Cain, Where is Abel thy brother? And he said, I know not; am I my brother's keeper? (Genesis 4:6-9).

Cain was upset because the Lord had respect for his brother Abel's offering, and Cain lied to God. So here we see the different evil spirits at work. We see those same old evil spirits ruling and reigning in people's lives today. The devil is a liar and tempter. God does not tempt any man! We can choose to resist the temptation because of the grace God has given us through His Son.

Blessed is the man that endureth temptation: for when he is tried, he shall receive the crown of life; which the Lord hath promised to them that love him. Let no man say when he is tempted, I am tempted of God. For God can not be tempted with evil, neither tempteth he any man. But every man is tempted, when he is drawn away of his own lust, and enticed. Then when lust hath conceived, it bringeth forth sin; and sin, when it is finished, bringeth forth death (James 1:12-15).

There hath no temptation taken you but such as common to man; but God is faithful, who will not suffer you to be tempted above that ye are able; but will with the temptation also make a way to escape, that ye may be able to bear it (I Corinthians 10:13).

Submit yourselves therefore to God. Resist the devil, and he will flee from you. Draw nigh to God, and he will draw nigh to you. Cleanse your hands, ye sinners; and purify your hearts, ye double-minded (James 4:7,8).

We must stay focused on our walk with Jesus. Remember Satan is constantly setting snares and traps for us. We do not have to fall into his pitfalls. The greater One lives inside of you. Satan had you once, do not let him trick you again.

Receive the Lord into your heart by faith. If you are struggling with any addictions or bondage, I pray for your deliverance right now in Jesus' name. Most of all, I pray for your salvation. Our Lord tells us to watch as well as pray. "Take ye heed, watch and pray; for ye know not when the time is" (Mark 13:33). Pray about everything.

In Christ we can have new life. We do not have to be

enslaved in bondage, and we do not have to live in fear. We do not have to be confused about who we are and the purpose for which we were born. "For God hath not given us the spirit of fear; but of power, and of love, and of a sound mind" (II Timothy 1:7).

If you are in need of deliverance, trust the Lord. Submit yourself to Him. Your deliverance may be a gradual deliverance, but keep trusting in the Lord and submitting to the Word of the Lord. God is able to deliver you. God wants you to be fruitful, healthy, and vibrant. God wants to work through you for His glory.

Learn to pray according to God's Word, and be obedient to your heavenly Father, and you can have what God says you can have. Faith and obedience to God are very important ingredients.

I pray that you will grow in all that the Lord has planned for your life. I pray that you will grow in the grace and fullness of Jesus Christ our Lord. I pray God's blessings upon every area of your life. I pray for you to be spiritually, emotionally, physically, mentally, and financially whole. I pray God's blessings to overtake you. I pray that your spiritual eyes will be opened and enlightened daily in Jesus' holy name.

Chapter 2

Jesus Sets Us Free

"And ye shall know the truth, and the truth shall make you free" (John 8:32).

When we accept Jesus Christ as our Lord and Savior, we do not have to walk and live in lies and bondages. Jesus Christ paid the price for our freedom. Jesus went to the cross and paid the penalty for our sins.

> *...by his own blood he* [Jesus] *entered in once into the holy place, having obtained eternal redemption for us* (Hebrews 9:12).

Jesus Christ paid the price for our sins once and for all. Jesus' blood was the perfect sacrifice shed on the cross at Calvary. The Blood of Jesus still saves lives.

In the Old Testament, "The high priest could enter the Holy of Holies, the innermost room of the tabernacle (Hebrew 9:3,7) one day each year to atone for Israel's sins. The Holy of Holies was a small room that contained the ark of the covenant (a gold-covered chest holding the original stone tablets on which the Ten Commandments were written, a jar of manna, and Aaron's staff). The top of the chest served as the altar on which the blood would be sprinkled by the high priest on the day of atonement. The Holy of Holies was the most sacred spot on earth for the Jews, and only the high priest could enter. The people's only access to God was through the high priest, who would offer a sacrifice and use the animal's blood to atone first for his own sins and then for the people's sins" (*Life Application Study Bible* NASB, Zondervan).

In the Old Testament, God chose Israel to be His chosen people, a people set apart for Himself to show forth His righteousness and His laws. When Israel sinned against God in the Old Testament, blood sacrifices were required to atone for their sins. "Atone" means to cover or cancel. In the Old Testament, righteousness was by works, but sinful man could not obey God's Law and meet God's righteous demands. Thank God for Jesus Christ.

When we accept Jesus Christ as our Lord and Savior, we obtain free access to God through Jesus Christ, and we do not have to depend on a high priest to present a sacrifice for the atonement of our sins.

> *How much more shall the blood of Christ, who through the eternal Spirit offered himself without spot to God, purge your conscience from dead works to serve the living God?* (Hebrews 9:14).

The Lord's blood is powerful enough to cleanse our conscience from dead, polluted, and wrong thinking. Jesus' blood is powerful enough to cover our sins.

> *For Christ is not entered into the holy places made with hands, which are the figures of the true; but into heaven itself, now to appear in the presence of God for us* (Hebrews 9:24.)

Jesus is our high priest. He is our advocate, and we can stand in His righteousness. God is holy. God dislikes sin but loves the sinner. God wants us to obey Him because only He truly knows what is best for us. Thank God for Jesus Christ our Lord. When we accept Jesus into our hearts by faith, God sees the blood of Jesus Christ over us.

> *Wherefore he is able also to save them to the uttermost that come unto God by him, seeing he ever liveth to make intercession for them* (Hebrews 7:25).

We can go to God in Jesus' name and receive forgiveness for our sins. Salvation comes through repenting of our sins and asking Jesus Christ to come into our heart by faith. When we repent, we are saying that we are going to turn from our sinful lifestyle to serve The True and Living God. God translates us from the kingdom of darkness into the kingdom of light, from being a sinner to being a saint.

Jesus Christ is light. The light of God's written Word has the power to drive out darkness in every area of our lives. The truth of God's holy Word will set us free, if we want to be free .

"If the son therefore shall make you free, ye shall be free indeed" (John 8:36). Jesus Christ is the one who has the power to set us free in every area of our lives, but we have to do our part and allow God's Holy Spirit to lead, guide, teach, and correct us. We must apply the Word of God to our lives daily. The Bible is God's instruction book for us to live by, and obedience to God is essential. "I will instruct thee and teach thee in the way thou shalt go: I will guide thee with mine eye" (Psalm 32:8). God wants to be our guide but we must yield to Him. God loves us and cares about us, and He wants His children to walk in victory.

"But God commendeth his love toward us, in that, while we were yet sinners, Christ died for us" (Romans 5:8). God did not have to make a way for us to be free from the power of sin, but because God is so good, merciful, and loving, He did make a way for us to walk in victory.

"There is therefore now no condemnation to them which are in Christ Jesus, who walk not after the flesh, but after the Spirit" (Romans 8:1). God wants us to walk in His Spirit, and to do that, Jesus said we must be born again.

> *Nicodemus saith unto him, How can a man be born when he is old? can he enter the second time into his mother's womb, and be born? Jesus answered, Verily, verily, I say unto thee, Except a man be born of water and of the Spirit, he cannot enter into the kingdom of God. That which is born of the flesh is flesh; and that which is born of the Spirit is spirit* (John 3:4-6).

Flesh and blood cannot enter into the Kingdom of God. "God is a Spirit: and they that worship him must worship Him in Spirit and in truth" (John 4:24). Our carnal mind cannot receive the things of the Spirit. Only the mind of the spirit can receive from God. "But the natural man receiveth not the things of the Spirit of God; for they are foolishness unto him; neither can he

know them, because they are spiritually discerned"
(I Corinthians 2:14).

Renewing Our Minds

God wants to talk to us through His Word. God's
Word is Spirit and life, but if we are not born again by
the Spirit of God, we will not understand what God
wants to say to us. Apostle Paul wrote to the church of
God at Corinth saying,

> *But as it is written, Eye hath not seen, nor ear
> heard, neither have entered into the heart of
> man, the things which God hath prepared for
> them that love him. But God hath revealed them
> unto us by his Spirit: for the Spirit searcheth all
> things, yea, the deep things of God. Now, we
> have received, not the spirit of the world, but
> the spirit which is of God; that we might know
> the things that are freely given to us of God*
> (I Corinthians 2:9-10,12).

God wants us to know Him. God also wants us to
know what He has freely given us in Jesus Christ. God
does not want us to be walking around in spiritual darkness. We must learn to give our minds and hearts to God
and allow Him to give us revelation through His Holy
Spirit. God can do a better job with our minds than we
can. God's Holy Spirit will help us to live the life that
God is calling us to live.

> *I beseech you therefore, brethren, by the mercies
> of God that ye present your bodies a living sac-
> rifice, holy, acceptable unto God, which is your*

*reasonable service. And be not conformed to this
world: but be ye transformed by the renewing of
your mind, that ye may prove what is that good,
and acceptable, and perfect, will of God*
(Romans 12:1-2).

It is time to change the scenes in our minds; it is
time for some new chapters to begin. Let's conform to
God's ways, renew our minds, and pursue the good, acceptable, and perfect will of God for our lives.

We have to learn how to crucify our flesh daily. Our
flesh seeks to entrap us by tempting us to give into un-
healthy desires that are in opposition with what God
tells us to do. Apostle Paul, wrote to the church in
Rome, "Knowing this that our old man is crucified with
him [Jesus Christ] that the body of sin might be de-
stroyed, that henceforth we should not serve sin"
(Romans 6:6). We have to crucify this flesh. Our flesh
wants to control us, but we do not have to give into the
flesh. When God gives us His Holy Spirit, we receive
power to resist the sinful desires of our flesh. We have to
choose whom we will follow. God does not dominate our
will, but He gives us the ability to choose between following Him or following our own fleshy impulses and desires. God wants us to cooperate with Him so that we
can walk in the light and life of His Son, Jesus Christ. If
we choose to walk outside of God's will for our lives,
then we are choosing to walk in spiritual darkness. Let
the old unregenerated man of the flesh die, and let's live
in the newness of life in Christ Jesus, the "New Man."

Now if we be dead with Christ, we believe that

we shall also live with him, knowing that Christ being raised from the dead dieth no more: death hath no more dominion over him (Romans 6:8-9).

Jesus said, verily, verily, I say unto you, he that heareth my word, and believeth on him that sent me, hath everlasting life, and shall not come into condemnation, but is passed from death unto life (John 5:24).

When we accept Christ as our Lord, we become children of God and joint heirs with Jesus Christ,

And if children, then heirs, heirs of God, and joint-heirs with Christ; if so be that we suffer with him, that we may be also glorified together. For I reckon that the sufferings of this present time are not worthy to be compared with the glory which shall be revealed in us (Romans 8:17-18).

Nothing we go through in this life can be compared with what is waiting for us in heaven. However, we can experience a little bit of heaven now on this earth if we learn how to walk in the spirit of Christ.

We can have a daily walk with Jesus Christ in which God's grace is available to help us. We must seek God's thoughts, His ways, His will, and His plan and purpose to be fulfilled and carried out in our lives daily.

We were created for God and by God. We must look to our Creator Father God for His plan to unfold in our lives. No one knows us like our heavenly Father. No one can take care of us like Him. When I was sinking deep in my sins, sinking as though to rise no more, God's unconditional love lifted me, and God's unconditional love wants to lift you!

Overcoming Sin

Sin will make us pay more than we want to pay. Sin will trap us and enslave us. Falling down is not a final failure, but staying down causes us to fail. The psalmist David said, "I will lift up mine eyes unto the hills, from whence cometh my help. My help cometh from the Lord, which made heaven and earth" (Psalm 121:1-2). We must keep looking towards the Lord because our help comes from Him.

Likewise reckon ye also yourselves to be dead indeed unto sin, but alive unto God through Jesus Christ our Lord. Let not sin therefore reign in your mortal body, that ye should obey it in the lusts thereof. Neither yield ye your members as instruments of unrighteousness unto sin: but yield yourselves unto God, as those that are alive from the dead, and your members as instruments of righteousness unto God (Romans 6:11-13).

A New Identity

God wants our heart to be established by His grace. In fact, God wants to give us a new heart.

A new heart also will I give you, and a new spirit will I put within you: and I will take away the stony heart out of your flesh, and I will give you an heart of flesh. And I will put my spirit within you, and cause you to walk in my statutes, and ye shall keep my judgements and do them (Ezekiel 36:26-27).

Therefore if any man be in Christ, he is a new creature; old things are passed away, behold all things are become new (II Corinthians 5:17).

All things will become new in us when we start doing new things in Christ. If we keep doing the same old things, we will keep getting the same old results, we'll remain in the same old lifestyle.

God wants us to walk in our new identity in Christ. We cannot live a holy life without God's Holy Spirit. Sometimes we will miss the mark, but thank God for Jesus Christ our Advocate. If we really desire to change, Father God will help us. If we really want to walk in our new identity in Christ, God will help us. We must have ears to hear and a heart to follow. Jesus said,

My sheep hear my voice, and I know them, and they follow me. And I give unto them eternal life; and they shall never perish, neither shall any man pluck them out of my hand (John 10:27-28).

God wants us to be sensitive to His voice. No one can pluck us out of His hand. God gives us His Holy Spirit and a new heart if we give Him our old heart. We are called to worship and thank God for who He is and what He has already done in our lives. We must admit that we cannot do anything without His guidance and wise counsel. We are called by God, and we are called to hear God speak to us through His Word.

Some of the things we need to do are: read the Bible daily, meditate upon God's word, go to church, go to Bible study, and be around other Christians so that we can grow strong and healthy in the things of God. God wants our bodies to be the temple of the Holy Ghost.

> *What? Know ye not that your body is the temple of the Holy Ghost which is in you, which ye have of God, and ye are not your own? For ye are bought with a price, therefore glorify God in your body, and in your spirit, which are God's"* (I Corinthians 6:19-20).

God wants each of His children to glorify Him in their bodies. God created us, and not we ourselves. We are called to seek those things which are above.

> *If ye then be risen with Christ, seek those things which are above, where Christ sitteth on the right hand of God. Set your affection on things above, not on things on the earth. For ye are dead, and your life is hid with Christ in God* (Colossians 3:1-3).

Let's seek to put our minds on the things of God. Our level of thinking will not rise until we pursue God's thoughts through the written Word of God. Our lives will not change until our level of thinking changes. God's holy Word has the power to transform our thoughts and our lives.

> *But seek ye first the kingdom of God, and his righteousness; and all these things shall be added unto you* (Matthew 6:33).

21

God is calling us to be kingdom seekers. seek God's kingdom, and all these other things will be added unto you. Seek to understand the ways of God.

> *The LORD looked down from heaven upon the children of men, to see if there were any that did understand, and seek God* (Psalm 14:2)..

We must seek God first and put Him at the top and center of all we do. We must surrender our will over to His will for our lives. When we allow God to govern our lives, real freedom will occur. When we begin to put God at the top of our list, everything else will fall into place.

God wants us to get holy in our minds, hearts, and spirits. God does not want us to be held in captivity to the negative influences around us. God does not want us to be addicted to anything except loving Him. We are called to love God and stay connected to Jesus.

> *Jesus said, I am the vine, ye are the branches; he that abideth in me, and I in him, the same bringeth forth much fruit; for without me ye can do nothing. If ye abide in me, and my words abide in you, ye shall ask what ye will, and it shall be done unto you. Herein is my Father glorified, that ye bear much fruit: so shall ye be my disciples* (John 15:5,7-8).

God wants us to bear the good fruit of peace, love, joy, gentleness, and self-control. God wants us to be healthy spiritually, mentally, and emotionally. We are told to think on good things

Be careful for nothing; but in every thing by prayer and supplication with thanksgiving let your requests be made known unto God. And the peace of God, which passeth all understanding, shall keep your hearts and minds through Christ Jesus. Finally, brethren, whatsoever things are true, whatsoever things are honest, whatsoever things are just, whatsoever things are pure, whatsoever things are lovely, whatsoever things are of good report; if there be any virtue, and if there be any praise, think on these things (Philippians 4:6-8).

Let this mind be in you, which was also in Christ Jesus (Philippians 2:5).

God does not want our souls to be bound by bitter, filthy, painful, and polluted memories from our past. God wants our souls and spirits free, cleansed, healed, and delivered so we can serve Him.

Freedom

Freedom comes in knowing who you are in Christ, and whose you are! For so many years I did not know what it meant to be free. I lived in mental, emotional, and physical bondage for so many years. From the age of 13-24, I lived an emotional, dry, and dependent life. My mind was being held in captivity, and I did not know that I was being held hostage within my own soul.

My soul was bound. It was bruised, wounded, trapped, and in pain. Emotional, mental, and physical bondage affects us all—the lower, middle, and upper class. There is no good thing in our flesh. We have no righteousness of our own, but because of what Jesus did at Calvary for us, we can stand in Jesus Christ's righteousness. "So then they that are in the flesh can not please God. Therefore, brethren, we are debtors, not to the flesh, to live after the flesh" (Romans 8:8,12).

That ye put off concerning the former conversation the old man, which is corrupt according to the deceitful lusts; and be renewed in the spirit of your mind. And that ye put on the new man, which after God is created in righteousness and true holiness (Ephesians 4:22-24).

The old man seeks to keep us in bondage and seeks to keep us living in the past. The new man in Christ wants to set us free and teach us how to live and walk in the truth of God's holy written Word.

For ye have not received the spirit of bondage again to fear; but ye have received the Spirit of adoption, whereby we cry, Abba, Father. The Spirit itself beareth witness with our spirit, that we are the children of God (Romans 8:15-16).

We are children of the Most High God if we have received Jesus Christ as our Lord.

And Jesus said unto them, I beheld Satan as lightning fall from heaven. Behold, I give unto you power to tread on serpents and scorpions, and over all the power of the enemy: and nothing shall by any means hurt you (Luke 10:18-19).

Freedom comes when we put our faith and trust in God. Freedom is knowing our true identity in Christ and having our soul anchored in the Lord. Freedom is knowing that when we pray, God is listening. Freedom is knowing that we are joint heirs of the kingdom of God. Freedom is knowing that we are doing the will of God in our lives. God's Word is liberating when we know Jesus Christ as our personal Lord and Savior. Freedom comes when we walk in what God says we can walk in. Freedom comes when we know that we are hearing God's voice through His written Word. Freedom comes when we stand firm in our identity in Christ. Freedom comes when we hear the truth of God's Word and apply it. Freedom in Christ liberates our soul and spirit

Are you free? Do you want to be set free? It is time to come and drink from Jesus' well.

But whosoever drinketh of the water that I shall give him shall never thirst; but the water that I shall give him shall be in him a well of water springing up into everlasting life (John 4:14).

Come to Jesus' well. There is plenty of fresh living water with which God wants to refresh your life. Jesus is the well that never runs dry. Jesus said,

I am that bread of life. Your fathers did eat manna in the wilderness, and are dead. This is the bread which cometh down from heaven, that a man may eat thereof, and not die. I am the living bread which came down from heaven; if any man eat of this bread, he shall live for ever; and the bread that I will give is my flesh, which I will give for the life of the world (John 6:48-51).

Jesus was talking to the Jews in the above verse. However, Jesus Christ is still the Bread of Life that came down from heaven, and we are commanded to eat the Bread of Life, the Word of God.

"Jesus said, It is written, Man shall not live by bread alone, but by every word that proceedeth out of the mouth of God" (Matthew 4:4). In order to live a healthy spiritual life, we must consume daily doses of God's written Word. If we do not eat and feast off the Word of God, we can become spiritually starved.

"Jesus said, I am the way, the truth, and the life; no man cometh unto the Father, but by me" (John 14:6). Jesus is the only way to develop a personal and intimate relationship with God our Creator.

"Thou shalt love the Lord thy God with all thy heart, and with all thy soul, and with all thy mind" (Matthew 22:37). God must be top priority. Everything that we are searching for is in God. God can satisfy our hungry hearts and our thirsty souls.

The Heart

My son, give me thine heart, and let thine eyes observe my ways (Proverbs 23:26).

Apply thine heart unto instruction, and thine ears to the words of knowledge (Proverbs 23:12).

God wants to clean out our hearts and remove everything from our hearts that isn't good and pure. God wants us to seek to have a clean pure heart. We have to get God's Word into our hearts daily. "Keep thy heart with all diligence; for out of it are the issues of life" (Proverbs 4:23). We have to guard our hearts. We must be aware of the television shows we watch and the music that we listen to because these things can affect us tremendously. The world's ways are in opposition with God's way. "For as he thinketh in his heart, so is he: Eat and drink saith he to thee; but his heart is not with thee" (Proverbs 23:7).

> *The heart is deceitful above all things, and desperately wicked; who can know it? The Lord search the heart. I try the reins, even to give every man according to his ways, and according to the fruit of his doings* (Jeremiah 17:9-10).

God knows everything that is in our hearts. God knows our motives, whether they are right or wrong. Nothing is hidden from God. King David was a man after God's own heart. In Psalm 51, King David wrote:

> *Have mercy upon me, O God, according to thy lovingkindness: according unto the multitude of thy tender mercies blot out my transgressions. Wash me thoroughly from mine iniquity, and cleanse me from my sin. Create in me a clean heart, O God, and renew a right spirit within me. Cast me not away from thy presence; and take not thy Holy Spirit from me. Restore unto me the joy of thy salvation; and uphold me with*

thy free spirit. Then will I teach transgressors thy ways; and sinners shall be converted unto thee. (Psalm 51:1-2,10-13).

We must ask God to give us a clean heart because most of us have a lot of junk from our past stored there. Confess to God and by faith receive your clean heart and right spirit in Jesus' holy name.

The Word

For the word of the Lord is right, and all his works are done in truth. By the word of the Lord were the heavens made; and all the host of them by the breath of his mouth (Psalm 33:4,6).

The Word of God is powerful and creative. We must learn to speak the Word of God over our circumstances.

For the word of God is quick, and powerful, and sharper than any two-edged sword, piercing even to the dividing asunder of soul and spirit, and of the joints and marrow, and is a discerner of the thoughts and intents of the heart (Hebrews 4:12).

The Word cleans us. Jesus said, "Now ye are clean through the word which I have spoken unto you" (John 15:3). "Sanctify them through thy truth: thy word is truth" (John 17:17).

The Word of God is able to heal and deliver us. "He sent his word, and healed them, and delivered them from their destructions" (Psalm 107:20).

"Thy word is a lamp unto my feet, and a light unto

my path. The entrance of thy words giveth light; it giveth understanding unto the simple" (Psalm 119:105, 130). The Word of God can guide us and keep us from the steps leading to darkness. The Word of God will light our paths.

This book of the law shall not depart out of thy mouth: but thou shalt meditate therein day and night, that thou mayest observe to do according to all that is written therein; for then thou shalt make thy way prosperous, and then thou shalt have good success. Have not I commanded thee? Be strong and of a good courage; be not afraid, neither be thou dismayed; for the Lord thy God is with thee whithersoever thou goest (Joshua 1:8-9).

Meditation upon the Word of God is important because it helps us to absorb the truth into our mind and spirit.

When we follow God's instructions, we will make our way prosperous, and then we will have good success.

For my thoughts are not your thoughts, neither are your ways my ways, saith the Lord. For as the Heavens are higher than the earth, so are my ways higher than your ways, and my thoughts than your thoughts (Isaiah 55:8-9).

We must understand that God does not think like us. We must seek to learn and understand God.

Chapter 3

God's Love

For God so loved the world, that he gave his only begotten Son, that whosoever believeth in him should not perish, but have everlasting life. For God sent not his Son into the world to condemn the world; but that the world through him might be saved (John 3:16-17).

God's love came down to us so that we would know his love. The cross is about the power of God's love. God's love is unconditional and everlasting towards us, and nothing can separate us from the love of God.

Who shall separate us from the love of Christ? Shall tribulation, or distress, or persecution, or famine, or nakedness. or peril, or sword? Nay, in all these things we are more than conquerors through him that loved us.

For I am persuaded that neither death, nor life, nor angels, nor principalities, nor powers, nor things present, nor things to come, nor height, nor depth, nor any other creature, shall be able to separate us from the love of God, which is in Christ Jesus our Lord (Romans 8:35, 37-39).

When I was out there in the world doing my own thing, my sins separated me from God, but the love of God drew me into His loving arms. God looked beyond my messed up life and saw my need. My need was to be saved by a loving, merciful, and gracious God. God sees your needs, and God wants you to rest in his loving arms too.

There is a story in the Bible about one brother and two sisters that Jesus loved. Their names were Martha, Mary, and Lazarus. When Lazarus became gravely ill, Mary and Martha sent word to Jesus.

> *Now Jesus loved Martha, and her sister, and Lazarus. When he had heard therefore that he [Lazarus] was sick, he abode two days still in the same place where he was. Then after that saith he to his disciples, Let us go to Judea again* (John 11:5-7).

> *Then said Jesus unto them plainly, Lazarus is dead. Then said Martha unto Jesus, Lord, if thou hadst been here, my brother had not died* (John 11:14,21).

> *Jesus said unto her, I am the resurrection, and the life; he that believeth in me, though he were dead, yet shall he live; and whosoever liveth and believeth in me shall never die. Believest thou this?* (John 11:25-26).

God is omnipresent. God is everywhere. God is omnipotent, all-powerful, and omniscient. God knows everything. God has already worked it out while we are still trying to figure it out. Whatever your "it" is, God's timing is not our timing. Lazarus died so that the glory and power of God could be shown. Jesus raised Lazarus from the dead so that those encamped around Him would believe that God had sent Him. Jesus has power over life and death. Whatever we go through in this life, we must learn to wait on God. Jesus wants to be glorified in you.

> *Wait on the Lord; be of good courage, and he shall strengthen thine heart; wait, I say, on the Lord* (Psalm 27:14).

No matter what your situation is and no matter how dead, hopeless, and dark it may seem, remember God knows everything. Nothing can separate you from the love of God in Christ Jesus. Just one word from the Master is all it takes. Jesus has the power and authority to cause us to get up, come forth, and be loosed.

During the dark years of my life, I was so deep into drugs, depression, and hopelessness that I could not see my way out. Satan who is the god of this world had blinded my mind. The scriptures says, "In whom the god of this world hath blinded the minds of them which believe not, lest the light of the glorious gospel of Christ, who is the image of God, should shine unto them" (II Corinthians 4:4).

God in his great love, mercy, and grace shined his light upon me. "For God, who commanded the light to shine out of darkness, hath shinned in our hearts, to give the light of the knowledge of the glory of God in the face of Jesus Christ" (II Corinthians 4:6).

God shined his light into my heart and taught me how to love and trust Him in everything.

God's love healed me, and God's love wants to heal you. Jesus came to heal the brokenhearted and to set the captives free.

And he [Jesus] came to Nazareth, where he had been brought up; and, as his custom was, he went unto the synagogue on the sabbath day, and stood up for to read. And there was delivered unto him the book of the prophet Esaias. And when he had opened the book, he found the place where it was written,

The Spirit of the Lord is upon me, because he hath anointed me to preach the gospel to the poor; he hath sent me to heal the brokenhearted, to preach deliverance to the captives, and recovering of sight to the blind, to set at liberty them that are bruised, to preach the acceptable year of the Lord (Luke 4:16-19).

Transformation occurs when we step over into the light and life of Jesus Christ. After the power, love, and light of the Lord shines into our heart, we will be set free and God will give us a new perspective about ourselves and the world in which we live. In our society today, we have some that are calling wrong right and right wrong.

Woe unto them that call evil good, and good evil;
that put darkness for light, and light for dark-
ness; that put bitter for sweet, and sweet for
bitter (Isaiah 5:20).

God loves us so much that He gave us the Bible to be
the standard for how we are to live the Christian life. A
Christian is a believer and follower of Jesus Christ. The
Gospel is about the good news of Jesus Christ. The good
news is that Jesus died, was buried, and rose from the
dead to deliver us from the power of sin. That's good
news, and that's the love of God manifested towards us.
The Gospel is about the love of God. "But if our gospel
be hid, it is hid to them that are lost" (II Corinthians
4:3).

For the preaching of the cross is to them that
perish foolishness; but unto us which are saved,
it is the power of God. Where is the wise? Where
is the scribe? Where is the disputer of this
world? Hath not God made foolish the wisdom
of this world? For after that in the wisdom of
God, the world by wisdom knew not God, it
pleased God by the foolishness of preaching to
save them that believe. Because the foolishness
of God is wiser than men: and the weakness of
God is stronger than men.

But God hath chosen the foolish things of the
world to confound the wise; and God hath
chosen the weak things of the world to confound

34

the things which are mighty. And base things of the world, and things which are despised, hath God chosen, yea, and things which are not, that no flesh should glory in his presence. But of him are ye in Christ Jesus, who of God is made unto us wisdom, and righteousness, and sanctification, and redemption; that, according as it is written, he that glorifieth, let him glory in the Lord (I Corinthians 1:18, 20-21, 25, 27-31).

The Lord is not slack concerning his promise, as some men count slackness; but is longsuffering to us-ward, not willing that any should perish, but that all should come to repentance (II Peter 3:9).

For all have sinned, and come short of the glory of God (Romans 3:23).

For God so loved the world, that he gave his only begotten Son that whosoever believeth in him should not perish, but have everlasting life (John 3:16).

Jesus was sent by God into the world for us, so we would not have to be lost. Jesus fulfilled His earthly mission successfully. Jesus is now sitting at the right hand of Father God.

God said, Let us make man in our image, after our likeness: and let them have dominion over the fish of the sea, and over the fowl of the air, and over the cattle, and over all the earth, and over every creeping thing that creepeth upon the earth. So God created man in his own image, in the image of God created he him; male and female created he them (Genesis 1:26-27).

God created man with an intellect, emotions and a will. God created us to have fellowship with Him. God created man to be upright and righteous, but the first man, Adam, sinned. Adam and Eve disobeyed God, and sin entered the world. We live in a fallen world because of this sin.

God does not have a physical body; He is Spirit. God is the ultimate supreme Power. We are human beings; God created us a little lower than the angels.

Thou madest him a little lower than the angels; thou crownedst him with glory and honour, and didst set him over the works of thy hands (Hebrews 2:7).

As it is written, There is none righteous, no, not one (Romans 3:10).

When we come into contact with Jesus Christ, we come into contact with truth, holiness, and righteousness. Jesus' Blood places us in right standing with God. GOD IS HOLY!

Jesus laid down His life for us at the cross to give us the wonderful privilege to become the children of God.

We are all God's creation, but when we repent of our sins and ask Jesus to come into our hearts by faith, we become the children of God. That's love. Jesus came into the world as a Light and laid down His life for the world.

Therefore doth my Father love me, because I lay down my life, that I might take it again. No man taketh it from me, but I lay it down of myself. I have power to lay it down, and I have power to take it again. This commandment have I received of my Father (John 10:17-18).

He that believeth on him is not condemned; but he that believeth not is condemned already, because he hath not believed in the name of the only begotten Son of God. And this is the condemnation, that light is come into the world, and men loved darkness rather than light, because their deeds were evil.

For everyone that doeth evil hateth the light, neither cometh to the light, lest his deeds should be reproved. But he that doeth truth cometh to the light, that his deeds may be made manifest, that they are wrought in God (John 3:18-21).

The night is far spent, the day is at hand. Let us therefore cast off the works of the darkness, and let us put on the armour of light (Romans 13:12).

God knows what is best for us, and He loves us and wants us to come to Jesus who is the light of the world. Jesus said, "I am the light of the world; he that followeth me shall not walk in darkness, but shall have the light of life" (John 8:12).

"And God said, Let there be light; and there was light" (Genesis 1:3). Receive the light and love of Jesus into your heart right now by faith in Jesus' name!

Love God!

"We love him, because he first loved us" (I John 4:19). Jesus said, "Thou shalt love the Lord thy God with all thy heart, and with all thy soul, and with all thy mind" (Matthew 22:37).

What is on the altar of your heart? I had many little gods on the altar of mine. Little gods can be whatever you worship, whatever you put before The True and Living God. For example: money, materialism, a job, a car, children, a man or a woman, etc. How foolish I was to put my faith and trust in those little gods of drugs and men. "Thou shalt have no other gods before me" (Exodus 20:3).

Trust!

"Trust in the Lord with all thine heart; and lean not unto thine own understanding" (Proverbs 3:5). "It is better to trust in the Lord than to put confidence in man" (Psalm 118:8). "The Lord redeemeth the soul of his servants; and none of them that trust in him shall be desolate" (Psalm 34:22). God is faithful!

Know therefore that the Lord thy God, he is God, the faithful God, which keepeth covenant and mercy with them that love him and keep his commandments to a thousand generations (Deuteronomy 7:9).

God is faithful, and He is a covenant keeping God. He never breaks His promises but is faithful to His Word.

God is faithful, by whom ye were called unto the fellowship of his Son Jesus Christ our Lord (I Corinthians 1:9).

Peace!

God gives His children peace. When I was in the world serving the devil and my flesh, I never had real peace. When the Lord began to give me his peace, I felt a little strange because I was so used to my mind wandering all over the place. My mind is sound and peaceful now, thank the Lord. I enjoy this peaceful mind that the Lord has given me.

Jesus is the Prince of Peace. "Thou wilt keep him in perfect peace, whose mind is stayed on thee; because he trusteth in thee" (Isaiah 26:3).

Jesus said, "These things I have spoken unto you, that in me ye might have peace. In the world, ye shall have tribulation; but be of good cheer; I have overcome the world" (John 16:33).

For unto us a child is born, unto us a son is

*given; and the government shall be upon his
shoulder; and his name shall be called
Wonderful, Counsellor, The mighty God, The
everlasting Father, The Prince of Peace* (Isaiah
9:6).

"The Lord will give strength unto his people; the
Lord will bless his people with peace" (Psalm 29:11).
After the Lord gave me His love and peace, God put His
joy into my heart. God wants you to have His joy in your
heart too. I pray right now that the joy of Jesus Christ
will flood your soul and your heart right now in Jesus'
holy name.

*Thou wilt shew me the path of life; in thy pres-
ence is fulness of joy; at thy right hand there are
pleasures for evermore* (Psalm 16:11).

*For his anger endureth but a moment; in his
favour is life; weeping may endure for a night,
but joy cometh in the morning* (Psalm 30:5).

Seek the Lord!

*And they that know thy name will put there
trust in thee; for thou, Lord hast not forsaken
them that seek thee* (Psalm 9:10).

*O, God, thou art my God; early will I seek thee;
my soul thirsteth for thee, my flesh longeth for
thee in a dry and thirsty land; where no water
is. To see thy power and thy glory, so as I have*

*seen thee in the sanctuary. Because thy lov-
ingkindness is better than life, my lips shall
praise thee. Thus will I bless thee while I live. I
will lift up my hands in thy name.*

*My soul shall be satisfied as with morrow and
fatness; and my mouth shall praise thee with
joyful lips. When I remember thee upon my bed,
and meditate on thee in the night watches.
Because thou hast been my help, therefore in the
shadow of thy wings will I rejoice. My soul followeth hard after thee; thy right hand upholdeth
me* (Psalm 63:1-8).

*The young lions do lack, and suffer hunger; but
they that seek the Lord shall not want any good
thing* (Psalm 34:10).

*When thou saidest, seek ye my face; my heart
said unto thee, thy face, Lord, will I seek* (Psalm
27:8).

Chapter 4

God's Grace and Mercy

But none of these things move me, neither count I my life dear unto myself, so that I might finish my course with joy, and the ministry, which I have received of the Lord Jesus, to testify the gospel of the grace of God (Acts 20:24).

When we are going through afflictions, storms, trials, and tribulations, we must be like Apostle Paul and stand firm in our faith in the Lord Jesus Christ and declare, "None of these things move me." When storms, tribulations, and trials come our way, and we feel like we are unable to deal with them, we must press into God more than ever. Storms can be an opportunity for us to grow closer to God and to build our character.

God gave us grace when He gave us Jesus Christ, His only begotten Son. We can make it through every storm that comes our way when we know Jesus Christ is in the storm with us.

In the beginning was the Word, and the Word was with God, and the Word was God. The same was in the beginning with God. All things were made by him; and without him was not

any thing made that was made. In him was life;
and the life was the light of men. And the light
shineth in darkness; and the darkness compre-
hended it not. And the Word was made flesh,
and dwelt among us, (and we beheld his glory,
the glory as of the only begotten of the Father)
full of grace and truth (John 1:1-5,14).

God's grace and truth are always near to help us through the storms, trials, and tribulations that we may face in this life. We must stand firm in our beliefs and continue in God's process of transformation for our lives. We must not allow our sinful nature to rule us during those times. We can overcome, and we can go through with Christ.

The Garden of Eden

We were born into sin because of Adam and Eve's disobedience in the garden of Eden, but God's grace came to us. God's grace gives us the power to overcome. We must remember that God created us to be winners in Christ.

Nevertheless death reigned from Adam to Moses,
even over them that had not sinned after the
similitude of Adam's transgression, who is the
figure of him that was to come [Jesus Christ].
But not as the offence, so also is the free gift. For
if through the offence of one many be dead,
much more the grace of God, and the gift by
grace, which is by one man, Jesus Christ, hath
abounded unto many (Romans 5:14-15).

*Therefore as by the offence of one judgment
came upon all men to condemnation; even so by
the righteousness of one the free gift came upon
all men unto justification of life. For as by one
man's disobedience many were made sinners,
so by the obedience of one shall many be made
righteous* (Romans 5:18-19).

Sin and death are reigning in the old creation in
Adam, but grace and righteousness are reigning in the
new creation over which Jesus Christ is the Head. If we
are born again Christians, we are in Christ. We are the
righteousness of God, and God has equipped us to win.
Grace is the outpouring of God's love and strength to us
that will enable us to do what we could not ordinarily do
in our own ability and strength.

God demonstrated through Jesus Christ that His
mercy and grace are great toward us. Jesus Christ came
to this earth for us, and at the age of 33, He went to the
cross for our sins. Jesus paid a debt that He did not owe,
and we owe a debt that we could never pay. Jesus
cleared us at the cross.

Jesus' journey here on the earth was not what you
would call pleasant. The prophet Isaiah wrote the following description about Jesus.

*He is despised and rejected of men; a man of
sorrows, and acquainted with grief: and we hid
as it were our faces from him; he was despised,
and we esteemed him not. Surely he hath borne
our griefs, and carried our sorrows: yet we did
esteem him stricken, smitten of God, and af-
flicted. But he was wounded for our transgres-*

sions, he was bruised for our iniquities: the chastisement of our peace was upon him; and with his stripes we are healed. All we like sheep have gone astray; we have turned every one to his own way; and the LORD hath laid on him the iniquity of us all (Isaiah 53:3-6).

When I look at what Jesus Christ went through during His earthly journey here on earth for us, I see the abundance of God's grace and mercy towards sinful humanity. Jesus paid the ultimate price to redeem us from sin and eternal separation from God. God has given us His power to triumph over sin. When we feel tempted and weak, we must remember that God has made an escape for us through His available grace.

"But as many as received him [Jesus], to them gave he power to become the sons of God, even to them that believe on his name" (John 1:12). Jesus gives us power to overcome the temptation to sin. "If we confess our sins, he is faithful and just to forgive us our sins, and to cleanse us from all unrighteousness" (I John 1:9).

Seeing then that we have a great high priest, that is passed into the heavens, Jesus the Son of God, let us hold fast our profession. For we have not an high priest which cannot be touched with the feeling of our infirmities; but was in all points tempted like as we are, yet without sin (Hebrews 4:14-15).

God is our source, our joy, our peace, our sustainer, our refuge, our shield, our buckler, and our helper. God

will give us all we need when we need it. God's grace is
sufficient. "All the paths of the Lord are mercy and truth
unto such as keep his covenant and his testimonies"
(Psalm 25:10).

"He shall send from heaven, and save me from the
reproach of him that would swallow me up. Selah. God
shall send forth his mercy and his truth" (Psalm 57:3).
This is a comforting scripture written by King David
when he fled from Saul in the cave.

The Lord is gracious and full of compassion;
slow to anger, and of great mercy (Psalm 145:8).

Who is a God like unto thee, that pardoneth in-
iquity, and passeth by the transgression of the
remnant of his heritage? He retaineth not his
anger for ever, because he delighteth in mercy
(Micah 7:18).

Jesus said, "Blessed are the merciful; for they
shall obtain mercy" (Matthew 5:7).

God expects His children to be merciful.

Then came Peter to him, and said, Lord, how oft
shall my brother sin against me, and I forgive
him? till seven times? Jesus saith unto him, I
say not unto thee, Until seven times: but, Until
seventy times seven. Therefore is the kingdom of
heaven likened unto a certain king, which
would take account of his servants. And when
he had begun to reckon, one was brought unto

him, which owed him ten thousand talents. But forasmuch as he had not to pay, his lord commanded him to be sold, and his wife, and children, and all that he had, and payment to be made. The servant therefore fell down, and worshipped him, saying, Lord, have patience with me, and I will pay thee all. Then the lord of that servant was moved with compassion, and loosed him, and forgave him the debt. But the same servant went out, and found one of his fellowservants, which owed him an hundred pence: and he laid hands on him, and took him by the throat, saying, Pay me that thou owest. And his fellowservant fell down at his feet, and besought him, saying, Have patience with me, and I will pay thee all. And he would not: but went and cast him into prison, till he should pay the debt. So when his fellowservants saw what was done, they were very sorry, and came and told unto their lord all that was done. Then his lord, after that he had called him, said unto him, O thou wicked servant, I forgave thee all that debt, because thou desiredst me: Shouldest not thou also have had compassion on thy fellowservant, even as I had pity on thee? And his lord was wroth, and delivered him to the tormentors, till he should pay all that was due unto him. So likewise shall my heavenly Father do also unto you, if ye from your hearts forgive not every one his brother their trespasses (Matthew 18:21-35).

A few years ago I was not a very merciful person towards my husband, and neither was he toward me. You will read more about that in chapter five. Thanks be to God for His grace that will enable us to give mercy. Thank you, God, for Your mercy towards us.

God has given us His kind and compassionate treatment, even though we did not deserve it. God demonstrated His mercy towards us at the cross. God is a God of mercy. He appeared to Moses in the cloud in Exodus 34:5-6.

And the LORD descended in the cloud, and stood with him there, and proclaimed the name of the LORD. And the LORD passed by before him, and proclaimed, The LORD, The LORD God, merciful and gracious, longsuffering, and abundant in goodness and truth.

Mercy is one of God's attributes, and God expects His children to be merciful.

Nevertheless for thy great mercies' sake thou didst not utterly consume them, nor forsake them: for thou art a gracious and merciful God (Nehemiah 9:31).

Not by works of righteousness which we have done, but according to his mercy he saved us, by the washing of regeneration, and renewing of the Holy Ghost (Titus 3:5).

"For he shall have judgment without mercy, that

hath shewed no mercy; and mercy rejoiceth against judgment" (James 2:13). Be merciful. Mercy triumphs over judgment.

> *But he giveth more grace. Wherefore he saith, God resisteth the proud, but giveth grace unto the humble. Submit yourselves therefore to God. Resist the devil, and he will flee from you. Draw nigh to God, and he will draw nigh to you. Cleanse your hands, ye sinners; and purify your hearts, ye double minded* (James 4:6-8).

God does not want us to be double-minded. we cannot serve God and the devil at the same time. We are called to walk humbly with God. We can pray and tell God about all of the areas that we need help in because God knows about those weaknesses anyway. God wants to give us His grace to overcome. God is a loving heavenly Father who wants to help His children to become all that He has created us to become in Him.

Submit yourself to your heavenly holy Father and surrender your will over to Him. Trust God to work in every area of your life by the power of His Holy Spirit, His Word, grace, and mercy. Trust God to change you from the inside out by the power of grace.

> *For by grace are ye saved through faith; and that not of yourselves: it is the gift of God: Not of works, lest any man should boast. For we are his workmanship, created in Christ Jesus unto good works, which God hath before ordained that we should walk in them* (Ephesians 2:8-10).

We are saved by grace through faith. We cannot work to obtain God's grace; God gives us His grace through faith in believing in His only begotten Son Jesus Christ. However, we were created unto good works. Good works do not justify us, but justified people do work.

"But wilt thou know, O vain man, that faith without works is dead?" (James 2:20).

> *Therefore being justified by faith, we have peace with God through our Lord Jesus Christ. By whom we also have access by faith into this grace wherein we stand, and rejoice in hope of the glory of God* (Romans 5:1-2).

God gives us his peace, and we have access to God by faith in Jesus Christ. We have access to God's grace and God wants us to stand in Christ and rejoice in hope to the glory of God.

God is our source, and only He is to be worshipped. We cannot afford to be disconnected from God in these dark and evil days. So much is going on in this world. We need the power of God intervening in our lives daily. We need the power of God's Word abiding in our hearts and spirits daily.

> *For whatsoever things were written aforetime were written for our learning, that we through patience and comfort of the scriptures might have hope* (Romans 15:4).

> *But the God of all grace, who hath called us unto his eternal glory by Christ Jesus, after that*

ye have suffered a while, make you perfect, establish, strengthen, settle you. To him be glory and dominion for ever and ever. Amen (I Peter 5:10-11).

Grace and peace be multiplied unto you through the knowledge of God, and of Jesus our Lord, According as his divine power hath given unto us all things that pertain unto life and godliness, through the knowledge of him that hath called us to glory and virtue: Whereby are given unto us exceeding great and precious promises: that by these ye might be partakers of the divine nature, having escaped the corruption that is in the world through lust. And beside this, giving all diligence, add to your faith virtue; and to virtue knowledge; And to knowledge temperance; and to temperance patience; and to patience godliness; And to godliness brotherly kindness; and to brotherly kindness charity. For if these things be in you, and abound, they make you that ye shall neither be barren nor unfruitful in the knowledge of our Lord Jesus Christ (2 Peter 1:2-8).

"Cast not away therefore your confidence, which hath great recompense of reward" (Hebrews 10:35). Be confident in who you are in Christ! "For all the promises of God in him are yea, and in him Amen, unto the glory of God" (II Corinthians 1:20). "Let us therefore come boldly unto the throne of grace, that we may obtain mercy, and find grace to help in time of need" (Hebrews 4:16).

Chapter 5

We Need "Now" Faith!

Have faith in God *now*. It is time to soar like an eagle and ride on the wings of faith. It is time to start believing the Word of God even before we see the manifestation. The woman with the issue of blood had the "now" faith.

> *And a certain woman, which had an issue of blood twelve years, and had suffered many things of many physicians, and had spent all that she had, and was nothing bettered, but rather grew worse, when she had heard of Jesus, came in the press behind, and touched his garment, for she said, If I may touch but his clothes, I shall be whole.*

> *And straightway the fountain of her blood was dried up, and she felt in her body that she was healed of that plague. And Jesus, immediately knowing in himself that virtue had gone out of him, turned him about in the press, and said, "Who touched my clothes?" And his disciples said unto him, "thou seest the multitude thronging thee, and sayest thou, who touched me?" And he looked round about to see her that had done this thing, but the woman fearing and*

trembling, knowing what was done in her, came and fell down before him, and told him all the truth. And he Jesus said, "Daughter, thy faith hath made thee whole; go in peace, and be whole of thy plague" (Mark 5:25-34).

In the book of Leviticus, this woman would have been considered unclean because of her issue of blood, and if anybody touched her, they would have been considered unclean also (Leviticus 15:19).

This woman had an issue of blood for 12 years. She probably had experienced some mental and emotional distress because of her situation. This woman probably felt lonely, hopeless, helpless, and rejected by society. She had spent all that she had trying to find some relief and get healed. She went to many physicians, but no doctor could help her. No person could help her.

This woman ran out of her resources. She probably wondered how she was going to make it from one day to the next. She heard that Jesus Christ was in her country. HOPE and FAITH came alive in her. She had heard about all the miracles that he had performed. She had heard that Jesus Christ specialty was in turning hopeless and helpless situations around. She heard that Jesus Christ had healed the sick, raised the dead, calmed the storms, and could fix the mind.

HOPE came alive in this woman. Her FAITH started working the moment she heard that Jesus was near. She had already made up in her mind, "If I may touch but his clothes, I shall be whole." She had the "NOW FAITH." "NOW FAITH is the substance of things hoped for, the evidence of things not seen" (Hebrews 11:1).

She knew that she needed to have her own personal

encounter with Jesus The Christ, The Anointed One. But she also knew that she needed to step out and act on her faith. So she pressed through the crowd and touched the hem of Jesus' garment. At that moment, virtue flowed from Jesus Christ to her. "She touched Jesus, and the healing power of God touched her back."

Jesus turned around and asked, "Who touched my clothes?" The disciples wanted to know how Jesus had known that someone had touched him in the midst of such a crowd. Jesus knew that someone touched him because faith gets Jesus attention! The woman fell down before Jesus and told Jesus all the truth.

Jesus was moved by her faith and said unto her, "Daughter thy faith hath made thee whole, GO IN PEACE, and be whole of thy plague." She knew that with God all things are possible!

> *But without faith it is impossible to please him;
> for he that cometh to God must believe that he
> is, and that he is a rewarder of them that dili-
> gently seek him* (Hebrews 11:6).

This woman believed in Jesus Christ in spite of her situation. This woman took her eyes off the problem and put her eyes on the solution, Jesus, The Christ, The Anointed One, The Healer, The Deliverer, Jesus The Lily of the Valley, Faithful and True, The Morning Star, Lord of Lords, King of Kings, Jesus, The Savior of the World. There is nothing too hard for God.

> *For with God nothing shall be impossible* (Luke
> 1:37).

Faith in Marriage

My husband and I had to stand in faith and believe God for us to have a successful marriage in Christ. We had to learn to believe God and the promises of God concerning our marriage, and as a result, we have been married for 10-1/2 years. I met my husband at a church I was attending where I was a part of the substance abuse ministry. Our ministry used to visit various hospitals and minister about the transforming power of the Gospel of Jesus Christ. The Lord saved and delivered my husband through that ministry. The night the Lord saved my husband, I was not present. My husband was saved and set free by the power of God on March 3, 1992. After my husband's three-day stay in the treatment center, he came home and joined the Substance Abuse Ministry. Every Friday night and Sunday morning my husband attended church. He began seeking God with all of his heart. After one year had passed, he approached me and said that it was God's will for us to be together. I prayed about it, and a few months later we were married. I would caution others about doing the same thing. I do not recommend this to anyone, however, this was how the Lord connected us together as husband and wife. Both of us loved God and wanted to live lives that would honor God and bring glory to Him. So we went through premarital counseling sessions, received the blessings of our pastor, and had a lovely wedding.

God overwhelmingly blessed us abundantly above all that we could ask or think. Everything just fell into place on that special day. That evening we went on our honeymoon, and the honeymoon was great. We came home from the honeymoon, and our struggles immediately began. I looked at him, and he looked at me, and we realized that we were truly different in every sense of the word. He had his own ways and ideas of doing things, and I had mine.

Our struggles continued for about 4 1/2 years. During this time, we found out that we were very selfish toward one another, and therefore struggled with becoming one. The word of God says,

> *Submitting yourselves one to another in the fear of God. Wives, submit yourselves unto your own husbands, as unto the Lord. For the husband is the head of the wife, even as Christ is the head of the church: and he is the saviour of the body. Therefore as the church is subject unto Christ, so let the wives be to their own husbands in every thing. Husbands, love your wives, even as Christ also loved the church, and gave himself for it; that he might sanctify and cleanse it with the washing of water by the word, that he might present it to himself a glorious church, not having spot, or wrinkle, or any such thing; but that it should be holy and without blemish. So ought men to love their wives as their own bodies. He that loveth his wife loveth himself. For no man ever yet hated his own flesh; but nourisheth and cherisheth it, even as the Lord the church: for we are members of his body, of his flesh, and of his bones. For this cause shall a man leave his father and mother, and shall be joined unto his wife, and they two shall be one flesh* (Ephesians 5:21-31).

During that time, I found out that I was not a spiritual super sister, and my husband discovered that he wasn't the strong awesome man of God, full of power. We lived in our home like strangers, and neither one of us wanted to die to self, and sacrifice for the other. My husband wanted things his way or no way, and I felt exactly the same way. We continued attending church and serving in our church. We were both struggling and unhappy with our marriage relationship. We had made a vow before God to glorify Him through our union, but we were not keeping our commitment to Him. We put on our happy faces at church, but when we left church it was another story. We treated other people better than we treated each other. Finally one day we realized, by the grace of God, that we needed to stop being disobedient in our marriage, repent, ask God for His forgiveness, and surrender to the instructions in the Word concerning our marriage. We surrendered. Although both my husband and I loved God and His Word, we realized that we really did not know how to become one, so I began buying books and tapes and asked God to help us with our marriage. We received counseling from about four different couples and attended various seminars. We did it all. By the power of God's Holy Spirit and Word, we both came to the realization that all we needed to do was surrender our will over to God's will, and practice and apply the Word of God to our problem area. We both had to stop blaming each other and focusing on each other's weaknesses and shortcomings. Instead, we began focusing on our Lord and released our faith in the Word of God.

We realized that we had to build our marriage based

on the Word of God and allow God's Holy Spirit to work in us and through us. We prayed and asked God to help us to see each other as He saw us. We prayed for healing, and as a result, we learned to respect each other and each other's opinions. We prayed for God's love to fill our hearts so that we could overflow with His love for each other. Because both of us were selfish, we wanted to hang onto our old ways of doing things. We were still looking at each other in the flesh and not through the eyes of the Spirit because we were not walking in the Spirit. We prayed to see each other through the eyes of the Holy Spirit. God taught us and continues to teach us how to surrender and submit to Him and to each other daily.

We both loved God, and we wanted God's plan fulfilled in our lives, but we did not want to surrender or submit to each other. However, we finally realized that God could not be pleased with our behavior. We came to a place where we said, "God, we surrender this area over to You in Jesus' holy name." We prayed and asked God to help us become one and build our marriage according to His Word.

For the past six years, my husband and I have truly learned to depend on God more, and love each other as never before. God has now blessed us with the ability to be best friends, good buddies, sister and brother in the faith, and most of all, husband and wife. God has helped us to experience many new and exciting things together. Not a day that goes by that my husband doesn't tell me how much he loves me. I truly admire and adore my husband, my man of faith, and a servant of The Most High God. God has blessed my husband with his own business, and I am his secretary. To God be the glory! We both have been blessed by God to minister together at substance abuse and detox facilities for men and women who are looking for deliverance from the Word of God.

If you are in a bad marriage, trust God to turn it around for His glory. "For with God nothing shall be impossible" (Luke 1:37). Have faith in God! If you are married and are hurting and struggling with your marriage, God wants you to know that He is well able to work your situation out. Take your eyes off the weaknesses of your man or woman and put them on Jesus Christ and the power of the Word. If you keep doing your part and ask God to help you to love and see your mate through His eyes, your marriage will be transformed. If you keep looking at all of the negative stuff, you will only make yourself miserable and thoroughly frustrated. Release your faith in God and do your part. Keep doing what God tells you to do concerning your mate even when you don't feel like it and trust God with the results. If you are not married, wait on God for a mate, and you will never go wrong. If you are married and have a great marriage, God bless you. I pray that you and your mate will continue to be all that God has created you to become in Him together representing His glorious Church.

God Can Do the Impossible!

"And this is the confidence that we have in him, that, if we ask anything according to his will, he heareth us" (I John 5:14). If you ask anything according to God's will, He hears you. That is good news! We must have "now faith."

And the Apostles said unto the Lord, Increase our faith. And the Lord said, If ye had faith as a grain of mustard seed, ye might say unto this sycamine tree, Be thou plucked up by the root, and be thou planted in the sea; and it should obey you (Luke 17:5-6).

Your mustard seed faith can allow you to do the impossible. Believe and have faith in God! How does faith come? "So then faith cometh by hearing, and hearing by the word of God" (Romans 10:17).

For I say, through the grace given unto me, to every man that is among you, not to think of himself more highly than he ought to think; but to think soberly, according as God hath dealt to every man the measure of faith (Romans 12:3).

God gives every man a measure of faith. Blind Bartimaeus had "now faith."

And they came to Jericho, and as he went out of Jericho with his disciples and a great number of people, blind Bartimaeus, the son of Timaeus, sat by the highway side begging. And when he heard that it was Jesus of Nazareth, he began to cry out, and say, Jesus, thou son of David, have mercy on me. And many charged him that he should hold his peace; but he cried the more a great deal, Thou son of David, have mercy on me (Mark 10:46-48).

We Need "Now" Faith!

The people charged blind Bartimaeus to be quiet, but Bartimaeus did not pay attention to them. He knew that it was his turn to be healed; it was his season. We cannot let anyone stand between us and our Savior. God wants to deliver us. When blind Bartimaeus heard that Jesus Christ was near, he knew that his deliverance had come. Although he had been viewed by society as the blind beggar, Jesus viewed him as a man of faith. We can't let our past or our present situation hold us back from reaching forth and stepping out in faith. Some of us need to let go of those old soul ties that seek to hold us from moving forward in Christ.

Bartimaeus was told to shut up, but he cried out even more. Just like Bartimaeus, we must not let anything or anyone stand in the way of our receiving from the Lord. "And Jesus stood still, and commanded him to be called, and they call the blind man, saying unto him, Be of good comfort, rise; he calleth thee" (Mark 10:49). Jesus commanded blind Bartimaeus to be called because faith gets the Lord's attention. The Lord wants us to cry out to Him.

> And he, casting away his garment, rose, and came to Jesus Christ. And Jesus answered and said unto him, What wilt thou that I should do unto thee? The blind man said unto him, Lord, that I might receive my sight. And Jesus said unto him, Go thy way; thy faith hath made thee whole. And immediately he received his sight, and followed Jesus in the way (Mark 10:50-52).

We do not have to allow what we did in our past to

61

dictate our future. Some of us have allowed the world in which we live in to shape and mold us. The good news is that God sees something in us that others cannot see with the natural eye. God sees what we can be in Jesus Christ, His only begotten Son. We do not have to walk in our past failures anymore. Bartimaeus received his sight, and a whole new life opened up for him. It does not matter if you have physical or spiritual blindness. Jesus Christ brings light to the situation whenever we come in contact with Him.

> *Remember ye not the former things, neither consider the things of old. Behold, I will do a new thing; now it shall spring forth; shall ye not know it? I will even make a way in the wilderness, and rivers in the desert* (Isaiah 43:18-19).

Our past can also hold us in bondage, so we need to let go of those soul ties that seek to hold us from moving forward in Jesus Christ. God wants to do a new thing in our lives. Sometimes we have to let go of the old to receive the fulness of the new.

"Call unto me, and I will answer thee, and shew thee great and mighty things, which thou knowest not" (Jeremiah 33:3). Do you want to see God's great and mighty power operating in your life? I do! Step out of the boat and pray for great and mighty things to be done in you and through you in Jesus' holy name.

> *And it came to pass, as he went to Jerusalem, he passed through the midst of Samaria and Galilee. And as he entered into a certain village,*

there met him ten men that were lepers, which stood afar off. And they lifted up their voices, and said, Jesus, master, have mercy on us. And when he saw them, he said unto them, Go shew yourselves unto the priests, and it came to pass, that, as they went, they were cleansed. And one of them, when he saw that he was healed, turned back, and with a loud voice glorified God. And fell down on his face at his feet, giving him thanks: and he was a Samaritan (Luke 17:11-16).

When God delivers us, we must remember to give Him the glory! God's thoughts toward us are ones of peace. He has a good future planned for us. We must look to Jesus the Author and Finisher of our faith, who for the joy that was set before him endured the cross, despising the shame, and is set down at the right hand of the throne of God.

In this world, we will go through trials, tribulations, and sickness, but Jesus still heals. We can take comfort in knowing that we do not have to go through anything alone. God is always near to give us peace in the midst of the storms, and God's healing power is still available to us. Give God the glory!

Have Faith in God!

My daughter, Lakeia, who is 23 years old now, had major surgery a year ago. Lakeia was diagnosed with epilepsy 11 years ago. She began having seizures. One day I took the kids to the mall. As I was walking in the parking lot, I noticed Lakeia smacking her hands. I called out to her, and she could not respond to me. The episode lasted for about three minutes. When she came to herself, she said that she was sleepy. Something strange had just happened to her, so I rushed her to the hospital. When we arrived at the emergency room, I told the nurses about the episode concerning my daughter. After a couple hours, the nurse finally called Lakeia to be seen by the doctor. When I explained to the doctor what had happened, he asked me if she had ever suffered with any type of mental illness, and I said no. He could not give me any explanation of what had just occurred. He gave me a referral to take her for a mental evaluation. I just looked at him helplessly and took the referral. He walked out of the office, and I began calling on God for help and answers. Immediately, Lakeia began to have another episode. I screamed for the doctor to come and witness the episode, and he was able to diagnose her as having partial complex seizures.

Lakeia was monitored in the hospital for about a week and a half. I prayed and prayed for the seizures to stop, but they just kept getting worse. I could have gotten bitter, but I decided to just trust God totally and believe that He would walk us through this difficult time. Lakeia would sometimes have up to 10 seizures a week. I took her to three different hospitals for all kinds of tests, evaluations, MRIs, and CAT scans. In the meantime Lakeia bravely continued going to school and did not allow her circumstances to cripple her. I witnessed Lakeia's faith grow in God. She did not allow those seizures to stop her from going to school. As a parent I would worry about this or that happening, but Lakeia was determined not to allow the seizures to interfere with her life.

Eventually, Lakeia graduated from high school and went to college in Richmond, Virginia for 1-1/2 years. While in college, Lakeia decided to have brain surgery— a left side lobectomy. This type of surgery was recommended by Lakeia's doctor because of the type of seizures she was having. She had a small portion of the left side of her brain removed where the seizure activity was occurring. The surgeon removed as much of the tissue as is medically possible without affecting other areas of the brain. Lakeia wanted to have this surgery because we were told that it was recommended for the type of seizures that she was having, and that she would be a good candidate for the surgery. Within 11 years, I have watched Lakeia's faith soar in the Lord. I watched her grow more and more dependent upon God to see her through this major problem. I watched first hand what it meant to trust God through a serious illness. Since the surgery, Lakeia still has about three to four episodes a month, but they only last about one minute. God started healing Lakeia gradually through her medication. Lakeia takes 16 pills a day, and she is still trusting God and believing Him for total deliverance. Today, Lakeia is still a college student, and she has high spirits.

God can heal supernaturally or God can heal in the natural through medication. Jesus Christ is still the great Physician. We trust Him totally and completely. Lakeia believes the Word of God, and she knows that God is with her. Even though our lives were interrupted with this illness, we had to keep on moving forward in God. We had to keep on believing and trusting that God knew about everything that we were going through. God wants us to know that He is with us. We can trust Him completely and totally with our lives.

God's grace is sufficient. God is still God, and God is still in control. Apostle Paul wrote,

> *For this thing I besought the Lord thrice, that it might depart from me. And He said unto me, "My grace is sufficient for thee; for my strength is made perfect in weakness, most gladly therefore will I rather glory in my infirmities, that the power of Christ may rest upon me. Therefore I take pleasure in infirmities, in persecutions, in distresses for Christ sake: For when I am weak, then am I strong"* (2 Corinthians 12:8-10).

Yes, I believe in healing, and I know God can heal our physical bodies. Yes, we have fasted, prayed, touched, agreed, and called up prayer partners for Lakeia. God is omnipotent, omnipresent, and omniscient. God is able to give us His grace, peace, love, and strength to walk us through whatever we may encounter in this life. God can turn our midnight into noonday. God can turn our darkness into bright sunshine when we just trust Him, thank Him, and praise Him. God's grace is sufficient to them that love and trust Him in all things.

> *Be careful for nothing; but in everything by prayer and supplication with thanksgiving let your request be made known unto God. And the peace of God, which passeth all understanding shall keep your hearts and minds through Christ Jesus. Finally brethren, whatsoever*

things are true, whatsoever things are honest, whatsoever things are just, whatsoever things are pure, whatsoever things are lovely, whatsoever things are of good report; if there be any virtue, and if there be any praise, think on these things (Philippians 4:6-8).

Chapter 6

To Dream Again

Joseph, one of Jacob's 12 sons, was obviously the favorite. Hated by his brothers for this, Joseph was sold to slave traders only to emerge as ruler of all Egypt. Through Joseph, we learn how suffering, no matter how unfair, develops strong character, and deep wisdom.

And Joseph dreamed a dream, and he told it his brethren; and they hated him yet the more. And he said unto them, hear, I pray you, this dream which I have dreamed, For behold, we were binding sheaves in the field, and lo, my sheaf arose, and also stood upright: and, behold, your sheaves stood round about, and made obeisance of my sheaf. And his brethren said to him, Shalt thou indeed reign over us? or shalt thou indeed have dominion over us? And they hated him yet the more for his dreams, and for his words. And he dreamed yet another dream, and told it his brethren, and said, Behold, I have dreamed a dream more: and, behold, the sun and the moon and the eleven stars made obeisance to me. And he told it to his father, and to his brethren: and his father rebuked him, and said unto him,

To Dream Again

What is this dream that thou hast dreamed?
Shall I and thy mother and thy brother indeed
come to bow down ourselves to thee to the
earth? (Genesis 37:5-10).

Jacob sent Joseph out to see how his brothers were getting along with the flocks. Joseph went looking for his brothers and found them. "And when they saw him afar off, even before he came near unto them, they conspired against him to slay him. And they said one to another, Behold, this dreamer cometh" (Genesis 37:18-19).

"And it came to pass, when Joseph was come unto his brethren that they strip Joseph out of his coat, his coat of many colours that was on him" (Genesis 37:23).

And Judah said unto his brethren, what profit is
it if we slay our brother, and conceal his blood?
Come, and let us sell him, to Ishmaelites, and let
not our hand be upon him; for he is our brother
and our flesh, and his brethren were content.
Then there passed by midianites merchant men;
and they drew and lifted up Joseph out of the
pit, and sold Joseph to the Ishmaelites for
twenty pieces of silver; and they brought Joseph
into Egypt. And the Midianites sold him into Egypt unto Potiphar, an officer of pharaohs, and captain of the guard (Genesis 37:26-28,36).

We never have to worry about others treating us wrongly. God sees everything, and no one gets away with anything. If someone mistreats us, they may think that they will get away with it, but vengeance belongs to God.

If it be possible, as much as lieth in you, live peaceably with all men. Dearly beloved, avenge not yourselves, but rather give place unto wrath: for it is written, Vengeance is mine; I will repay, saith the Lord (Romans 12:18-19).

God can bless us no matter where we are at. We are not so distant that God does not know our address. God is able to bless us with His favor, and open doors that have been shut. God is able to touch hearts and minds to get His blessings through to us. God has blessings with our name on it. We must be obedient to God and do what is right in His sight.

Potiphar's Wife Framed Joseph

And it came to pass after these things, that his master's wife cast her eyes upon Joseph; and she said, Lie with me. But he refused, and said unto his master's wife, Behold, my master wotteth not what is with me in the house, and he hath committed all that he hath to my hand; There is none greater in this house than I; neither hath he kept back any thing from me but thee, because thou art his wife: how then can I do this great wickedness, and sin against God? (Genesis 39:7-9).

Joseph had godly fear for the Lord. He was a man of integrity and great character. Joseph knew right from wrong and did not want to engage in any conduct that would mess up his witness for the Lord. Joseph knew that he was a man of destiny and promise and that the hand of the Lord was upon his life. Men and women of God should not give themselves to immoral conduct. Our bodies are to be the temple of God. We are to glorify God with them in every area of our lives. God created marriage and sex for a married union between a man and a woman. We grieve God's Holy Spirit when we have sexual contact outside of marriage. If you find yourself being tempted sexually by a man or a woman flee as Joseph did. God will give you the strength and grace to do so.

Although Joseph did the right thing, He was framed anyway. Truth always prevail, but it might take some time to come forth—"Be sure your sin will find you out" (Numbers 32:23).

> *He that planted the ear, shall he not hear? he that formed the eye, shall he not see?* (Psalm 94:9)

> *Am I a God at hand, saith the Lord, and not a God afar off? Can any hid himself in secret places that I shall not see him? saith the Lord. Do not I fill Heaven and earth? saith the Lord* (Jeremiah 23:23-24).

Sometimes it may seem that we were in the wrong place at the wrong time, and sometimes we may encounter situations that we may not have caused. But, if we are sincere about our walk with Jesus Christ, God is able to keep us safe during both the good times and the difficult times, even if we are falsely accused as Joseph was. God is still in control.

When we desire to walk uprightly before the Lord and do what is right in His sight, God will bless us and pour His favor upon us in the midst of what seems to be an uncomfortable place.

God never forgot Joseph or all that he endured. Joseph suffered in prison because of Potiphar's wife, but in the end, he was released and given the second highest in the land. Do not worry about grabbing recognition, promotion comes from the Lord. God knows us and remembers our good deeds.

> *And the Lord was with Joseph, and he was a prosperous man: and he was in the house of his master the Egyptian. And his master saw that the Lord was with him, and that the Lord made all that he did to prosper in his hand. And Joseph found grace in his sight, and he served him; and he made him overseer over his house, and all that he had put into his hand.* (Genesis 39:2-4).

If God is for us, who can be against us? God is looking for people whom he can work through and show himself strong through by the power of His precious Holy Spirit, but we have to learn to cooperate with God and His plan for us. God has a good plan for our lives, but without a test there is no testimony. Without a trial, there is no victory.

Joseph had been envied by his brothers, thrown in a pit, sold into slavery, lied about by pharaoh's wife, thrown into prison, and betrayed. However, God was with Joseph every step of the way, and the hand of the Lord was upon him. People plotted to get rid of him, but in spite of all that, Joseph persevered, knowing that his strength came from the Lord. Man did not call Joseph. Joseph was called out by God for a special purpose.

God knew Joseph's beginning and his end. God had a plan for Joseph's life; God He has a plan for ours. God knows our beginning and our end. No matter what we go through, we must believe in the dreams and visions that God has birthed in our spirit and heart. We must keep looking at the promise and not at the problems. For every problem we go through, there is a promise from the Word of the Lord. However, we must be careful about whom we share our dreams with because there are people who are dream killers. If God has given us a dream, we must hold onto it, nurture it, speak about it, write it down, and believe that God will bring it to pass. If we can dream it because God gave it to us, then we can have it. If we can see the dream, we can have it.

And when all the land of Egypt was famished, the people cried to Pharaoh for bread: and Pharaoh said unto all the Egyptians, Go unto Joseph; what he saith to you, do. And the famine was over all the face of the earth: and Joseph opened all the storehouses, and sold unto the Egyptians; and the famine waxed sore in the land of Egypt. And all countries came into Egypt to Joseph for to buy corn because that the famine was so sore in all lands (Genesis 41:55-57).

Now, guess who had to come back and pay Joseph a visit? Guess who had to end up being fed by Joseph?

Now when Jacob saw that there was corn in

Egypt, Jacob said unto his sons, Why do ye look one upon another? And he said, Behold, I have heard that there is corn in Egypt: get you down thither, and buy for us from thence; that we may live, and not die. And Joseph's ten brethren went down to buy corn in Egypt (Genesis 42:1-3).

God blessed Joseph abundantly and eventually took care of his entire family through him. Joseph stayed on course and came out better. Joseph was a man of destiny and he knew it in spite of all his mishaps. When we stick to the plan, we can watch God work it out.

Joseph always kept a compassionate heart. He had many opportunities to be bitter, but he overcame evil with good. The Lord was with Joseph, and everyone around him knew it. Although Joseph's brothers did all kinds of evil things to him, Joseph provided for them in their time of need. God had already planned for Joseph's future, and today God has our future planned. God wants us to come out better and not bitter. We must keep doing what we know is right in the sight of God, no matter what those around us are doing..

For I know the thoughts that I think towards you, saith the Lord, thoughts of peace, and not of evil, to give you an expected end. Then shall ye call upon me, and ye shall go and pray unto me, and I will hearken unto you. And ye shall seek me, and find me, when ye shall search for me with all your heart (Jeremiah 29:11-13).

And we know that all things work together for

good to them that love God, to them who are called according to his purpose (Romans 8:28).

To love God we must know God. And we know God through His holy written Word and spending time with God in prayer. God can take what the devil meant for evil and turn our bad experiences around for His glory. We must desire to do right and live right before God. God is to be glorified through our witness for him. God has the power, authority, and ability to carry out His plan.

God is not a man, that he should lie, neither the son of man, that he should repent; hath he said, and shall he not do it? or hath he spoken, and shall he not make it good? (Numbers 23:19).

Trust in the Lord, and do good, so shalt thou dwell in the land, and verily thou shalt be fed. Delight thyself also in the Lord; and he shall give thee the desires of thine heart. Commit thy way unto the Lord; trust also in him; and he shall bring it to pass (Psalm 37:3-5).

It's okay to dream again, only this time God wants to birth us with His divine dreams for his glory, honor, and praise. What dreams and visions has the Lord given you? What desires has God placed in your heart for His purpose and glory?

Gifts

God has given all of us gifts and talents to be used for

good to help strengthen the body of Jesus Christ and to minister to those in the workplace and community to bring glory, honor, and praise to Him.

> *So we, being many, are one body in Christ, and every one members one of another having then gifts differing according to the grace that is given to us, whether prophecy, let us prophesy according to the proportion of faith; or ministry, let us wait on our ministering, or he that teacheth, on teaching, or he that exhorteth, on exhortation: he that giveth, let him do it with simplicity; he that ruleth, with diligence; he that sheweth mercy, with cheerfulness* (Romans 12:5-8).

"Now there are diversities of gifts, but the same Spirit. And there are diversities of operations, but it is the same God which worketh all in all" (I Corinthians 12:4,6). God has given each of us gifts and talents in the body of Christ. He wants us to be helpers of one another. We are to nurture each other's gifts for the furtherance of the Gospel of Jesus Christ. We all have been blessed with different gifts, but for one purpose—to work together in the body of Christ until we all come into the unity and knowledge of our Lord and Savior, Jesus Christ.

One gift is not better than another. We all are important to Father God. It is God's program, we must be willing to use what God has blessed us with to point people to Him.

> *For as the body is one, and hath many members, and all the members of that one body,*

being many, are one body; so also is Christ. If the foot shall say, because I am not the hand, I am not of the body; is it therefore not of the body? And if the ear shall say, Because I am not the eye, I am not of the body, is it therefore not of the body. If the whole body were an eye, where were the hearing? If the whole were hearing, where were the smelling? (I Corinthians 12:12,15-17).

Nay, much more those members of the body, which seem to be more feeble, are necessary: and those members of the body, which we think to be less honorable, upon these we bestow more abundant honor: and our uncomely parts have more abundant comeliness (I Corinthians 12:22-23).

We must pray and ask God to help us to develop the gifts He has given us for the building up of His kingdom.

Talents

For the kingdom of heaven is as a man traveling into a far country, who called his own servants, and delivered unto them his goods. And unto one he gave five talents, to another two, and to another one; to every man according to his several ability, and straightway took His journey (Matthew 25:14-15).

Talents were given among this man's servants according to their abilities; no one received more or less than he could handle. If he failed in his assignment, his

77

excuse could not be that he was overwhelmed. Failure could come only from laziness or hatred toward the master. The talents represent any kind of resource we are given. God gives us talents, gifts, and other resources according to our abilities, and expects us to invest our talents wisely until He returns. We are responsible to use well what God has given us. The issue is not how much we have, but how well we used what we have. It is okay to dream again! God has placed in us all gifts and talents to work for good and to bring glory and honor to God!

Chapter 7

To God Be the Glory!

And the Lord God formed man of the dust of the ground, and breathed into his nostrils the breath of life; and man became a living soul (Genesis 2:7).

Our breath belongs to God our Creator and heavenly holy Father. Let's exalt His name forever and ever.

Praise ye the Lord. Praise God in his sanctuary; praise him in the firmament of his power. Praise him for his mighty acts; praise him according to his excellent greatness. Praise him with a sound of the trumpet, praise him with the psaltery and harp. Praise him with the timbrel and dance; praise him with the stringed instruments and organs. Praise him upon the loud cymbals; praise him upon the high sounding cymbals. Let every thing that hath breath praise the Lord. Praise ye the Lord (Psalm 150:1-6).

When I consider thy heavens, the work of thy fingers, the moon and the stars, which thou hast ordained; What is man, that thou art mindful of

*him? and the son of man, that thou visitest him?
For thou hast made him a little lower than the
angels, and hast crowned him with glory and
honour. Thou madest him to have dominion over
the works of thy hands; thou hast put all things
under his feet. O Lord our Lord, how excellent is
thy name in all the earth!* (Psalm 8:3-6,9).

God is great, holy, and full of truth and righteousness. God created the stars and the moon. Everything
God created is good. "O give thanks unto the Lord; for
he is good; for his mercy endureth for ever" (Psalm
136:1). God's mercy is from everlasting to everlasting.

*To him who alone doeth great wonders; for his
mercy endureth forever. To him that by wisdom
made the heavens; for his mercy endureth for
ever. To him that stretched out the earth above
the waters; for his mercy endureth forever. To
him that made great lights; for his mercy endureth forever. The sun to rule by day; for his
mercy endureth forever. The moon and stars to
rule by night; for his mercy endureth for ever*
(Psalm 136:4-9).

*For the Lord taketh pleasure in his people; he
will beautify the meek with salvation. Let the
saints be joyful in glory; let them sing aloud
upon their beds. Let the high praises of God be
in their mouth, and a two-edged sword in their
hand* (Psalm 149:4-6).

To God Be the Glory!

Praise our God. All honor, glory, and praise belongs to God for He is clothed in majesty and power. Nothing can compare to the awesome wonder of our God. He rules and reigns from on high. Praise His Holy Name!

"Praise ye the Lord; for it is good to sing praises unto our God: for it is pleasant; and praise is comely" (Psalm 147:1).

He healeth the broken in heart, and bindeth up their wounds. He telleth the number of the stars; he calleth them all by their names. Great is our Lord, and of great power; his understanding is infinite.

Sing unto the Lord with thanksgiving; sing praise upon the harp unto our God. Who covereth the heaven with clouds, who prepareth rain for the earth, who maketh grass to grow upon the mountains (Psalm 147:3-5, 7-8).

Let us sing thanksgiving to our God, who has created the heaven and the clouds. Pray and ask God to put a new song into your heart; worship the King!

"The heavens declare the glory of God; and the firmament sheweth his handiwork. Day unto day uttereth speech, and night unto night sheweth knowledge" (Psalm 19:1-2).

"Sing forth the honour of his name; make his praise glorious. Say unto God, How terrible art thou in thy works: through the greatness of thy power shall thine enemies submit themselves unto thee" (Psalm 66:2-3). Sing glorious praises to our God, and tell God how awesome He is to you.

"Great is the Lord, and greatly to be praised; and his greatness is unsearchable. The Lord is righteous in all his ways, and holy in all his works" (Psalm 145:3,17). God's greatness is unsearchable, and God is righteous in all His ways. Holy is our King.

> *This I recall to my mind, therefore have I hope.*
> *It is of the Lord's mercies that we are not con-*
> *sumed, because his compassion fail not. They*
> *are new every morning: great is thy faithfulness.*
> *The Lord is my portion, saith my soul: therefore*
> *will I hope in him* [God]. *The Lord is good unto*
> *them that wait for him, to the soul that seeketh*
> *him* (Lamentations 3:21-25).

There is none like our King. God is great, awesome, holy, marvelous, powerful, all knowing, and a God of justice. God is all in all. God is the great I Am.

> *I will bless the Lord at all times; his praise shall*
> *continually be in my mouth. My soul shall make*
> *her boast in the Lord; the humble shall hear*
> *thereof, and be glad. O magnify the Lord with*
> *me, and let us exalt his name together. I sought*
> *the Lord, and he heard me, and delivered me*
> *from all my fears. They looked unto him and*
> *were lightened; and their faces were not*
> *ashamed. This poor man cried, and the Lord*
> *heard him, and saved him out of all his trou-*
> *bles. The angel of the Lord encampeth round*
> *about them that fear him, and delivered them. O*
> *taste and see that the Lord is good, blessed is the*
> *man that trusteth in him* (Psalm 34:1-8).

To God Be the Glory!

The Lord is nigh unto them that are of a broken heart; and saveth such as be of a contrite spirit. Many are the afflictions of the righteous; but the Lord delivereth him out of them all. He keepeth all his bones; not one of them is broken. The Lord redeemeth the soul of his servants; and none of them that trust in him shall be desolate (Psalm 34:18-20,22).

When thou passeth through the waters, I will be with thee; and through the rivers, they shall not overflow thee: when thou walkest through the fire, thou shalt not be burned; neither shall the flame kindle upon thee (Isaiah 43:2).

He giveth power to the faint, and to them that have no might he [God] increaseth strength. But they that wait upon the Lord shall renew their strength; they shall mount up with wings as eagles; they shall run, and not be weary; and they shall walk, and not faint (Isaiah 40:29,31).

God is able to gird us up with His strength. Refreshing and restoration is here. We can soar upon the Word of the Lord when we give God our weariness.

And the Lord shall guide thee continually, and satisfy thy soul in drought, and make fat thy bones: and thou shalt be like a watered garden, and like a spring of water, whose waters fail not (Isaiah 58:11).

Lead me in thy truth, and teach me; for thou art

the God of my salvation; on thee do I wait all the day. Remember, O Lord, thy tender mercies and thy loving kindness; for they have been ever of old. Remember not the sins of my youth, nor my transgressions; according to thy mercy remember thou me for thy goodness' sake, O Lord. Good and upright is the Lord; therefore will he teach sinners in the way (Psalm 25:5-8).

I will sing unto the Lord as long as I live: I will sing praise to my God while I have my being. My meditation of him shall be sweet; I will be glad in the Lord (Psalm 104:33-34).

How sweet are thy words unto my taste! Yea, sweeter than honey to my mouth. Through thy precepts I get understanding; therefore I hate every false way (Psalm 119:103-104).

We must keep eating the words of purity and of truth; we must get God's Word into our spirits and denounce every false way.

The law of the Lord is perfect, converting the soul: the testimony of the Lord is sure, making wise the simple. The statutes of the Lord are right, rejoicing the heart; the commandment of the Lord is pure, enlightening the eyes. The fear of the Lord is clean, enduring for ever: the judgments of the Lord are true and righteous altogether. More to be desired are they than gold , yea, than much fine gold: sweeter also than honey and the honeycomb (Psalm 19:7-10).

To God Be the Glory!

Thus saith the Lord, let not the wise man glory in his wisdom, neither let the mighty man glory in his might, let not the rich man glory in his riches; But let them that glorieth glory in this, that he understandeth and knoweth me, that I am the Lord which exercise loving kindness, judgment, and righteousness, in the earth. For in these things I delight, saith the Lord (Jeremiah 9:23-24).

We have nothing to glory in, all of our glorying is to be glorying in who God is and what God has done. We must glory in knowing, pursuing and understanding God. For these things God delights in!

I will love thee, O Lord, my strength. The Lord is my rock, and my fortress, and my deliverer; my God, my strength, in whom I will trust; my buckler, and the horn of my salvation, and my high tower. I will call upon the Lord, who is worthy to be praised; so shall I be saved from my enemies. In my distress I called upon the Lord, and cried unto my God; he heard my voice out of his temple, and my cry came before him, even into his ears (Psalm 18:1-3,6).

It is God that girdeth me with strength, and maketh my way perfect. He maketh my feet like hinds' feet, and setteth me upon my high places (Psalm 18:32-33).

Walking With God!

*Now the Lord had said unto Abram, Get thee out
of thy country, and from thy kindred, and from
thy father's house, unto a land that I will shew
thee: and I will make of thee a great nation, and
I will bless thee, and make thy name great; and
thou shalt be a blessing* (Genesis 12:1-2).

God is looking for a people that He can set apart for
His purposes. God wants us to learn to deny ourselves
because He has a higher purpose for our lives. God's purpose is for us to be an open and willing vessel that He
can work through to bring blessings to others that need
to hear about and receive His only begotten Son, Jesus
Christ, into their hearts by faith. God wants to bless us,
our children, and our children's children. God wants His
ways, righteousness, and truth to be passed down from
generation to generation.

When God instructs us to do something, it is because
He has an assignment that He wants to accomplish
through us. We are blessed to be a blessing. Sometimes
we just need to go and pitch a tent before the Lord, and
just stay there, seek the face of the Lord, and call upon
His name. God wants us to be separated for His use. "Be
ye not unequally yoked together with unbelievers, for
what fellowship hath righteousness with unrighteousness? and what communion hath light with darkness?"
(II Corinthians 6:14).

We must be careful with whom we associate ourselves with, because some people will add to our life, and
some people will always seek to take away from our life.
It is important for us to invest our time wisely because

we are on a mission for God. Pray and ask God who He wants you to connect with.

Worship God and give God the highest praise with your life. Let your light shine in this dark world, and make a statement with your life. To God be the glory.

Arise, shine; for thy light is come, and the glory of the Lord is risen upon thee. For behold, the darkness shall cover the earth, and gross darkness the people; but the Lord shall arise upon thee, and his glory shall be seen upon thee (Isaiah 60:1-2).

God is saying arise! Arise, get up, and get moving! My light is upon thee! Arise and shine and carry my glory upon thee. The world is dark and I am calling you to be light and to carry my glory upon thee. Come out of darkness in every area of your life, and walk in the light of God's holy written word! Remember, you carry the promise within you, God's divine nature the precious Holy Spirit. Keep moving forward and keep walking with God.

The Prayer of Salvation

If you have read this book and you have never asked Jesus Christ to come into your heart, I pray that you will do so right now. Romans 10:9-11 says,

That if thou shalt confess with thy mouth the Lord Jesus, and shalt believe in thine heart that God hath raised him from the dead, thou shalt be saved. For with the heart man believeth unto righteousness; and with the mouth confession is made unto salvation. For the scripture saith, Whosoever believeth on him shall not be ashamed

Repeat after me, "Lord Jesus, I confess that I am a sinner, and I believe that You went to the cross for my sins. I believe that You died and rose on the third day. I receive Your forgiveness."

If you have accepted Jesus Christ as your Lord and Savior at some point in your life, and you have since walked outside of God's will for your life, pray and ask for God's forgiveness for the sins that you have committed against Him, in Jesus' holy name.

If you are saved and are walking with the Lord, God bless you in Jesus' holy name. May you continue to be built up in our Lord and strengthened day by day in your inner man. To God be the glory, forever and ever!

About the Author

Vernell Hightower is a born again child of The Most High God. She lives in Baltimore, Maryland, with her husband Tyrone. Vernell and Tyrone have been married for 10-1/2 years and are the owners of a home improvement business. They have a blended family, which consists of three young adult children—one son and two daughters. Vernell and Tyrone are a part of the substance abuse ministry in their church, and she is also a part of the women's prison ministry. Vernell has a passion to see people set free and delivered by the power of the written Word of God. She desires to see people move into a close intimate relationship with The True and Living God.

To contact the author:

Vernell Hightower
P.O. Box 66529
Baltimore, Maryland 21239-6529
Transforming power@jesusanswers.com